Experiments with MAGNETS AND METALS

Christine Taylor-Butler

Raintree

www.raintreepublishers.co.uk
Visit our website to find out more information about Raintree books.

To order:
☎ Phone 0845 6044371
🖷 Fax +44 (0) 1865 312263
🖳 Email myorders@raintreepublishers.co.uk

Customers from outside the UK please telephone +44 1865 312262

Raintree is an imprint of Capstone Global Library Limited, a company incorporated in England and Wales having its registered office at 7 Pilgrim Street, London, EC4V 6LB – Registered company number: 6695582

Text © Capstone Global Library Limited 2011
First published in hardback in 2011
Paperback edition first published in 2012
The moral rights of the proprietor have been asserted.

Edited by Rebecca Rissman, Dan Nunn, and Catherine Veitch
Designed by Richard Parker
Picture research by Tracy Cummins
Originated by Capstone Global Library
Printed in China

ISBN 978 1 406 22905 9 (hardback)
15 14 13 12 11
10 9 8 7 6 5 4 3 2 1

ISBN 978 1 406 22911 0 (paperback)
16 15 14 13 12
10 9 8 7 6 5 4 3 2 1

British Library Cataloguing in Publication Data
Taylor-Butler, Christine.
Experiments with magnets and metals. -- (My science investigations)
538'.078-dc22
A full catalogue record for this book is available from the British Library.

Acknowledgements
We would like to thank the following for permission to reproduce photographs: Alamy p. 29 (© ELC); Getty Images p. 6 (Michael Grecco Photography); Heinemann Raintree pp. 8, 10, 11, 12, 14, 15, 16, 17, 18, 19, 20, 21, 22, 24, 25, 26, 27 (Karon Dubke); istockphoto p. 28 (© Nikada); Nasa p. 4 (Visible Earth); Photolibrary p. 5 (© Leonard Lessin).

Cover photograph of a child holding a magnet reproduced with permission of Getty Images (Mike Kemp). Background photograph of metal reproduced with permission of Shutterstock (© caesart).

Special thanks to Suzy Gazlay for her invaluable help in the preparation of this book. We would also like to thank Ashley Wolinski for her help in the preparation of this book.

Every effort has been made to contact copyright holders of material reproduced in this book. Any omissions will be rectified in subsequent printings if notice is given to the publisher.

Contents

Magnets on Earth..4

How scientists work 6

Magnetic attraction? 8

Share the power.....................................12

The invisible force 16

Break the barrier...................................20

Pointing north 24

Your turn!..28

Glossary 30

Find out more 31

Index..32

Some words are printed in bold, **like this**.
You can find out what they mean by looking
in the Glossary.

Magnets on Earth

Earth's **magnetic** energy comes from deep within its **core**.

Earth is a giant magnet. One end is near the North Pole. The other is near the South Pole. Scientists study magnets and metals to learn more about our planet.

This lodestone is a powerful magnet.

Thousands of years ago, people discovered rocks that could pick up metal objects. These natural magnets are called **lodestones**.

How scientists work

Scientists start with a question about something they **observe**, or notice. They gather information and think about it. Then they make a guess, or **hypothesis**, about a likely answer to their question. Next they set up an **experiment** to test their hypothesis. They look at the **data**, or **results**, and make a decision, or **conclusion**, about whether their hypothesis is right or wrong.

There are many steps in a scientific experiment.

$$F = \frac{k_e q_1 q_2}{r^2}$$

How to do an experiment

1. Start a **log**. Write down your **observations**, question, and hypothesis.
2. Plan step by step how you can test the hypothesis. This is called the **procedure**.
3. Carry out the experiment. **Record** everything that happens. These are your observations.
4. Compare your results with your hypothesis. Was your hypothesis right or wrong? What did you learn? The answer is your conclusion.

observe

↓

hypothesis

↓

experiment

↓

data

↓

conclusion

↙   ↘

hypothesis true   hypothesis false

Magnetic attraction?

Magnets can **attract**, or pull, and **repel**, or push. This is called **magnetic force**. Magnets have two **poles**, a north pole and a south pole. The push and pull of a magnet are strongest at its poles.

Hypothesis

The two poles of a magnet behave in opposite ways.

You will need these things for your **experiment**.

Procedure

1. Place the south pole of a magnet next to the north pole of another magnet. **Observe**. Do the opposite ends attract?

2. Pull the magnets apart and put a finger between them. What happens? Try two fingers, then three. Keep going until the attraction stops. **Record** your **observations**.

Distance between magnets	What happens?
one finger's width	
two fingers' width	
three fingers' width	

Make a table like this in your **log** to record your **results**.

Float!

3. Turn one magnet so its south **pole** is on the right. Turn the second magnet so that its south pole is also on the right. Place the second magnet on top of the first one. What happens?

4. Push the magnets together and wrap with two strips of tape. Let go. What happens? **Record** your **observations**.

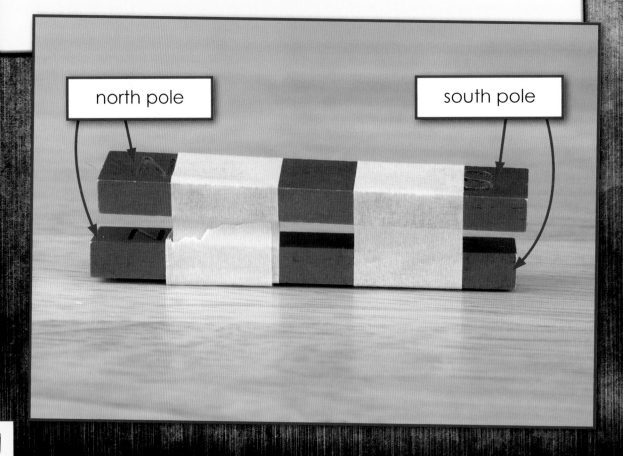

north pole

south pole

5. Try longer strips of tape. Does it still work? Record your observations.

The science explained

Opposite (north and south) poles **attract** each other. The same poles **repel**, or push, each other away.

How high can you make the top magnet float?

Share the power

Magnets **attract** some things, but not others. Will they attract any object made of metal?

Hypothesis

Magnets attract all metal objects.

Warning!

Collect some **materials** to test. Do not put magnets near computers, CDs, DVDs, or credit cards.

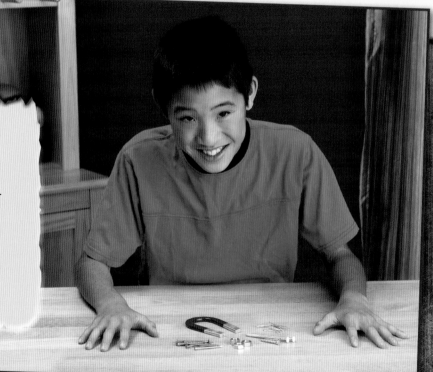

Procedure

1. Collect as many different metal objects as you can find.
2. Make a table with four columns. List the objects you collected in the first column.
3. Touch each metal object with a magnet. Put an X to show if it is attracted to the magnet a lot, a little, or not at all.

The science explained

Magnets do not attract all metals the same way. Iron and steel have a strong attraction. Others are attracted weakly or not at all.

Object	Attracted a lot	Attracted a little	Not attracted

Make a table like this in your **log**. You can list as many objects as you like!

Hypothesis

A stronger magnet will pick up more paperclips.

Things that can be **attracted** by a magnet are called **magnetic**.

Procedure

1. Use a magnet to pick up a paperclip. Touch the free end of the paperclip to another paperclip. What happens?

2. How many paperclips can you pick up in a chain? Try this several times. Each time, **record** the number you can pick up.

3. Repeat steps 1 and 2 with different magnets. Which magnet picks up the most paperclips?

Record how many paperclips you can pick up at a time.

The invisible force

Every magnet is surrounded by an area where its **force** is strongest. This area is called its **magnetic field**. We can't see a magnetic field, but we can see what the force of a magnet does.

Hypothesis

The shape of a magnetic field depends upon the shape of the magnet.

Collect these things for your **experiment**.

Procedure

1. Place a bar magnet underneath a sheet of paper.
2. Hold two steel wool pads a ruler's length above the paper. Rub the pads together. Let the pieces of steel wool sprinkle over the paper. Draw the pattern you see in your **log**.
3. Do the steel wool pieces stick to the paper? Gently shake the paper. Does the pattern change? **Record** your **observations**.

Steel wool is **magnetic**.

17

4. Repeat the **experiment** with a horseshoe magnet. What happens? Is the pattern the same or different? **Record** your **observations** in your **log**.

5. What is the shape of the **magnetic field** around each magnet? Where is the pull of the magnet the strongest? How do you know?

The science explained

The areas where the pull of the magnets is strongest attract the most bits of steel wool. The pattern of these pieces shows the shape of the magnetic field.

Break the barrier

A magnet can sometimes **attract magnetic** objects, even through something that is in the way.

Hypothesis – Part 1

A magnet will attract metal through paper or glass, but not through plastic or china.

You will need these things for your experiment.

Procedure

1. Place paperclips or nails inside a paper cup. Hold a bar magnet on the outside of the cup. Does it attract any clips or nails?

2. Repeat the **experiment** using a glass. Then try it with a plastic bowl and a china mug. Do you get the same **results**? **Record** your **observations**.

When you repeat an experiment, it's important to do exactly the same thing each time.

Hypothesis – Part 2

A magnet will **attract** metal objects through a few pages of a magazine, but not through the whole magazine.

Procedure

1. Put four or five clips or nails on a table.
2. Open a magazine so the cover rests on top of the metal objects. Place a magnet on top of the cover. What happens?

Do you think the magnet will attract all the metal objects?

3. Open the magazine at page 10. Rest these pages and the cover on top of the metal objects. Place a magnet on top of the cover. How many are still **attracted**?

4. Repeat with pages 20, 30, and so on. Finally, put the whole magazine on top of the clips or nails. Each time, **record** your **observations**.

The science explained

Magnetic force can go through some solid **materials**. Its strength depends upon what the materials are made of and how thick they are.

Number of pages	How many nails were attracted?
～～～	～～～
～～～	～～～
～～～	～～～

Make a table like this in your **log**.

Pointing north

The needle on a **compass** always points north. How does this happen? The compass needle is **magnetic**. Earth is a big magnet. The pull of its **magnetic field** causes the compass needle to point towards Earth's magnetic north **pole**.

With these simple **materials**, you can build your own compass!

Procedure

1. Draw a line about two finger's width from the bottom of a plastic cup. Cut along the line with scissors, all round the cup.

2. Place a bar magnet flat inside the bottom part of the cup.

3. Float the cup and magnet in a bowl of water. What happens to the cup? **Record** your **observations** in your **log**.

Be careful when you cut the plastic cup.

4. Push the cup to the opposite side of the bowl. What happens?

5. Turn the cup. Does it turn back? Does it return to the same spot? **Record** your **observations** in your **log**.

Try turning the bowl. Do the magnet and the cup turn, too?

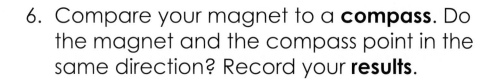

6. Compare your magnet to a **compass**. Do the magnet and the compass point in the same direction? Record your **results**.

Can you think of any other objects that could be turned into a compass?

Your turn!

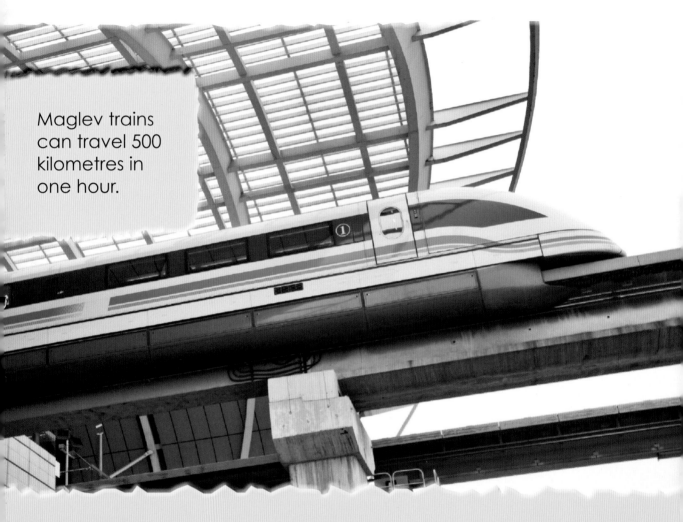

Maglev trains can travel 500 kilometres in one hour.

Scientists use magnets to make electricity. They also use magnets to make things move. A Maglev train uses giant magnets to float above its track, rather than move directly on the rails. It also gets its power from **magnetic forces**.

Can magnets make a toy move across the floor? Think of a way that can be done. What's your **hypothesis**? Design an **experiment** to test your idea.

Some toys are made of magnets.

Glossary

attract pull something towards an object

compass tool used to find directions

conclusion what you learn from the results of an experiment

core innermost part of Earth

data information gathered in an experiment

experiment organized way of testing an idea

force power to pull, push, or change something

hypothesis suggested statement or explanation that can be tested

lodestone type of rock that can attract metal

log written notes about an experiment

magnetic is a magnet and can attract some metals, or something that acts as a magnet

magnetic field area in which a magnet's forces act on magnetic objects

materials anything used for making something else

observe watch, or notice, something

observation something you notice, or observe, with any of your five senses

poles one of the two ends of a magnet, where the force is strongest

procedure steps followed to carry out an experiment

record draw or write something down

repel when objects push each other away

results what happens in an experiment

Find out more

Books

Magnet Power! (First Science Experiments), Leslie Johnstone and Shar Levine (Sterling Juvenile, 2006)

Magnets (Investigate), Sue Barraclough, Chris Oxlade, and Charlotte Guillain (Heinemann Library, 2008)

Magnets (My World of Science), Angela Royston (Heinemann Library, 2008)

Websites

www.bbc.co.uk/schools/ks2bitesize/science/ physical_processes/magnet_springs/read1. shtml
Visit this website to learn about magnets and springs, including a fun game and a quiz.

www.channel4learning.com/apps26/learning/ microsites/E/essentials/science/ physical/magnetssprings_bi.jsp
Learn about magnets and springs, with activities, key terms, and more on this website.

Index

attract 8, 9, 11, 12, 13, 14, 19, 20-23

bar magnets 17, 25

china 20, 21

compass 24, 27

compass needle 24

conclusions 6, 7

data 6, 7

Earth 4, 24

Earth's core 4

electricity 28

experiments 6-7

floating magnets 10-11, 28

glass 20, 21

horseshoe magnets 18

hypothesis 6

lodestones 5

log 7

Maglev trains 28

magnetic 14, 24

magnetic field 16-19, 24

magnetic force 4, 8, 16, 23, 28

metal objects 12-15, 20-23

nails 22-23

natural magnets 5

north and south poles 4, 8-11, 24-27

north, pointing 24-27

observations 6, 7

paper 20-21, 22-23

paperclips 14-15

plastic 20, 21

procedure 7

recording 7

repeating experiments 21

repel 8, 11

results 6, 7

scientists 6, 28

steel wool 17-19

toys 29